FOUR QUESTIONS

WORKBOOK

Your Strategy To Move Forward

KIM M. MAAS

TEN35
PRODUCTIONS

A Ten35 Productions Publication

kimmaas.com

Requests for information should be addressed to:

Ten35 Productions, *P.O Box 271, Moorpark, California 93020*

Layout and Design by Sabrina Schlesinger Graphic Design
Cover Artwork by Sabrina Schlesinger Graphic Design

Consultation editing and concept by
Hannah Lee
As One Strategy
http://asonestrategy.com/
hannah@asonestrategy.com

Printed in the United States of America

Table of Contents

Preface

This is the perfect time to move forward in God's dreams and vision for your life. It's not complicated. It begins with a strategy.

The Move Forward! Workbook and Move Forward! MP3 are designed to help you partner with the Holy Spirit to create your own personal strategy for moving forward in the God dreams and visions for your life.

You will be guided through various exercises and questions, listen for the still small voice, and make a personal commitment to action.

Dr. Kim Maas has taught this strategy creating course in many parts of the world, helping God's people to move forward in the call on their lives.

To download the free MP3 go to https://kimmaas.com/shop/fourquestions/ and at checkout use the code "Freemp3".

Introduction

My friends call me the Move Forward woman. It's true. It's true they call me this. And it is true that I move forward–every season. At the end of every season I have moved from where I was the season before.

We all do. The question is have we moved **forward**?

Let me ask you a few questions. How do you feel when you go to bed at night? Have you accomplished the things that are most important to you? Have you accomplished the things in line with who God says you are and has called you to do? What do you imagine it would feel like to know you accomplished those things for several days in a row? Where would you find yourself if you did that for a whole season?

Here are comments I hear from a lot of people:

A. My life feels out of control
B. I work so hard, but nothing seems to ever get done
C. I am busy all the time doing so many things, but I don't feel like I ever get to the things that are most important to me.
D. You always seem to move forward. *HOW DO YOU DO THAT?*

When I began walking in my call, I had a husband, three school-age children, and a full-time job. Yet, I managed to walk according to the call of God on my life. Let's get this straight right off the bat, I am NOT saying, "Pull yourself up by your own bootstraps." None of this can be accomplished in your own strength.

There are major parts to this call thing that only God can do. Yet, we do have a part to play. We do have a responsibility to shoulder. I am also not saying there haven't been times in my own walk when I *DID NOT* lift the tiniest finger to participate in what God was doing in my life. I have experienced deep discouragement, bone weariness, a health crisis, and intimidation so strong I have felt immobilized at times. Sometimes we fall down, get sick, or become exhausted. In these moments, we have to know that we know that we know God's love and grace is bigger!

I'm here to tell you, **YOU CAN DO IT!**

A few suggestions before you start:

1. Make room in your schedule—add an appointment in your calendar.
2. Allow for a whole day or a whole weekend. (It may take more than a single sitting to work through the workbook).
3. Don't worry if you don't have all the answers right away. Stay open before God.
4. Remember, progress not perfection. What you write can be adjusted or expanded later. Just start!

Get ready to **MOVE FORWARD**!

Dr. Kim Maas

Commitment

Commit your works to the LORD, and your plans will be achieved.
Proverbs 16:3

_____ I commit to this process to strategize for my next season with God.

_____ I have scheduled two days to work through this book.

_____ I have prayed through the process.

_____ I am open to hear what God has to say about my next season.

_____ Even if my words are not perfect, I commit to start and finish this process.

_____ I am ready to **Move Forward** into my next season.

Date _____ Name _____

Signature _____

Reflection on the past season

Before we ask questions about the new season, it is important for us to reflect on the past season. God is always working in our lives. Taking time to reflect on the past season allows us to clarify what He did, gain insight from it, and thank him for it.

Close your eyes and reflect upon the past season. Ask the Lord for a picture and draw the picture below.

Ask the Lord for an interpretation for what you saw and write it down below.

Is there anything new or surprising in what God showed you?

Write down some of the testimonies and victories from this past season.

Of all that transpired in the last season, of all that God accomplished in and through your life, which was the one that most inspired, encouraged, affirmed, and impassioned you? Why?

What were you doing when you experienced the most freedom and joy on the inside? What were you doing when you experienced the most favor and release on the outside from others?

Ask those around you to share:

    A. How and in what ways they have seen growth in your life?
    B. What ways they have seen God move in and through you this past season?
    C. Is there a victory or testimony from your life they feel should be celebrated?
    D. What do they see God highlighting for the future in your life?

My leaders:

_____

_____

_____

_____

_____

_____

_____

_____

_____

My peers:

_____

_____

_____

_____

_____

_____

_____

_____

_____

_____

_____

_____

My family:

_____

_____

_____

_____

_____

_____

_____

_____

_____

Those I lead:

_____

_____

_____

_____

_____

_____

_____

_____

_____

_____

_____

_____

Was there anything surprising in what your community shared with you?

_____

_____

_____

_____

_____

_____

_____

_____

_____

_____

What insights did you receive from hearing from your community?

_____

_____

_____

_____

_____

_____

_____

_____

_____

_____

_____

_____

_____

_____

How does it help or inspire you for next season?

What does God want to do in me?

Right now, God has a vision for our lives. He sees the future and what we are becoming. He sees the present and where we are at right now. We want to see our lives from His perspective so we can always be moving in the right direction; in the direction of His vision for us.

Who does God say you are?

How does God see you? Close your eyes and ask the Lord. Draw the picture that you see below.

Ask the Lord for interpretation of your vision and write it down below.

Is this different from the way you see yourself? How?

Greater intimacy with God allows you live more fully out of who you are. However, it is also reciprocal in that the more you become who God says you are, the more intimacy you will be able to have with Him. Your identity is specific to you and your calling not someone else.

Who is God calling you to be?

_____

_____

_____

_____

_____

_____

_____

_____

_____

_____

How would you describe your intimacy with the Lord right now?

_____

_____

_____

_____

_____

_____

_____

_____

_____

_____

_____

_____

Where do you want to be in terms of your intimacy with the Lord?

In this season...

God is interested in us, personally. He is interested in our relationship with Him, and our growth and development as His child. This first question also involves identity. Our true identity is formed by God, in relationship with Him. The more we become who God says we are, the more we mature and increase in our ability to co-labor with Him.

Close your eyes and reflect upon this upcoming season. Ask the Lord for a picture of how He wants to work in you this season and draw the picture below.

Ask the Lord for an interpretation for what you saw and write it down below.

Ask for help in the interpretation from your community and write those insights below.

_____

_____

_____

_____

_____

_____

_____

_____

_____

_____

What does God want you to allow Him to work on in your life this season, personally and individually?

_____

_____

_____

_____

_____

_____

_____

_____

_____

_____

_____

_____

In what specific area in your life does He want to bring change or transformation? Is it a habit? Is it a character issue? Is it a belief system or a false understanding? Is it an old reactive response pattern?

_____

_____

_____

_____

_____

_____

_____

_____

_____

What does He want to do (or change) in respect to your relationship with Him this season?

_____

_____

_____

_____

_____

_____

_____

_____

_____

_____

_____

_____

_____

Check in with your trusted leaders. Is there anything that they see in you that needs to grow, develop, change or be removed?

What does God want to do through me?

God is interested in us coming to understand the purpose and call upon our lives. Read the following verses and write down any insights you receive about them.

Matthew 28:18-20

Mark 16:15-18

Isaiah 60

Isaiah 61

We all have a call to reach others, dispel the works of darkness, proclaim and demonstrate the Gospel, and complete the mission of Christ on the earth until His return. What we are called to do is clear. How we do it is particular to each of us individually.

Whether Author, Business leader, Mother, Nurse, Teacher, Evangelist, or Prophet, in this next season what do we want to know of how God wants to work through our lives for others?

- Where will He send us?
- To whom and for what is He sending us?
- What is He desiring to accomplish in that place with those people for His purposes through us?

In this next season, what does He want to do through your life for others?

_____

_____

_____

_____

_____

_____

_____

_____

_____

_____

_____

_____

_____

_____

_____

_____

_____

_____

_____

Where does He want to send you?

_____

_____

_____

_____

_____

_____

_____

_____

_____

To whom, and for what is He sending you?

_____

_____

_____

_____

_____

_____

_____

_____

_____

_____

_____

Priorities and Boundaries

A river without banks is a flood. When water flows within banks on either side we call it a stream or a river. A river is full of twists and turns but is always going in the same direction with a single purpose-to reach the sea! Our lives are like a river. It is not meant to be purposeless or directionless like a flood. Our lives and personal resources are meant to flow in one direction, which is toward the fulfillment of God's will, promises, and dreams for our lives all the while empowered by the Holy Spirit.

Like banks to a river, priorities and boundaries keep us strong, focused and going in one direction-forward.

What priorities does God want me to set?

Read Matthew 6:24. What insights do you gain from this verse?

_____

_____

_____

_____

_____

_____

_____

_____

_____

_____

Priorities are the things you give your resources to. These include temporal, relational, physical, emotional, intellectual and financial resources. Reflecting upon the last season and where you spent your resources, what have your priorities been?

_____

_____

_____

_____

_____

_____

_____

_____

_____

_____

_____

_____

We all have the same amount of time in a day, a month, or a season. How we spend our time makes all the difference. We all have significant relationships to protect and value. We all have one physical body to care for. We all have a limited capacity for emotional and financial expenditure.

Priorities are those things we determine to truly value. Priorities are those things we hold as sacred; the things we will guard and protect as sacred.

What have you valued and guarded in the last season?

_____

_____

_____

_____

_____

_____

_____

_____

_____

_____

In this upcoming season, what will you need to put a high value on? What will you commit to guard in your life in order that God is able to do in and through you what He desires?

_____

_____

_____

_____

_____

_____

_____

_____

_____

_____

What priorities do I need to establish?

This season, I plan to set the following priorities

☐ ....

    So that ....

☐ ....

    So that ....

☐ ....

    So that ....

☐ ....

    So that ....

☐ ....

    So that ....

☐ ....

    So that ....

☐ ....

    So that ....

☐ ....

    So that ....

☐ ....

    So that ....

☐ ....

    So that ....

☐ ....

    So that ....

☐ ....

    So that ....

What are the boundaries God wants me to set?

We cannot keep our priorities if we do not have any boundaries. Remember, a river without banks is simply a flood. Read through the following verses and note your insights on the boundaries that Jesus kept.

Luke 2:49

_____

_____

_____

_____

_____

_____

_____

_____

_____

_____

_____

_____

_____

_____

_____

_____

_____

_____

_____

_____

John 5:19

John 5:1-6

Priorities are the things we give our attention and resources to. Boundaries are the things we don't. Boundaries help us discern what to say no to; things like distractions, the good but not best, unnecessary arguments, unproductive or abusive relationships, time-wasters (like computer games and TV), crisis that is not really crisis, the enemy. Without boundaries, priorities become muddled and eventually disappear.

It is as important to say NO as it is to say yes. ***LEARN TO SAY NO***!

Where does the enemy come and shift your attention?

Are there people or relationships in your life that are an unnecessary, unhealthy, or ungodly drain on your resources? What is God asking you to do (or NOT do) in regard to each of them?

_____

_____

_____

_____

_____

_____

_____

_____

_____

What unhealthy, time-wasting, or energy draining activities do you engage in that keep you from fulfilling your priorities?

_____

_____

_____

_____

_____

_____

_____

_____

_____

_____

_____

What boundaries do I need to establish?

This season, I plan to set the following boundaries.

☐ _____

    So that _____

☐ _____

    So that _____

☐ _____

    So that _____

☐ _____

    So that _____

☐ _____

    So that _____

☐ _____

    So that _____

☐ _____

    So that _____

☐ _____

    So that _____

☐ _____

    So that _____

☐ _____

    So that _____

☐ _____

    So that _____

☐ _____

    So that _____

The "WORD" for the Season

What one word describes what the Lord is saying to you, personally, about this season?

Now that you know what The Lord wants to do in and through you this season and the priorities and boundaries you will need to establish, it is time to condense it down to one single word. A single word is easy to remember. It will be the trigger word that brings to your remembrance all God has spoken to you through the previous pages in this workbook.

Take your time. Invite the Holy Spirit to bring the word to your mind and form the word in you.

Word:

Definition: (Use a dictionary and thesaurus)

Description: (Use your own words and describe what the word means to you as it pertains to what God wants to do in and through you. What comes to your mind when you hear this word? How does it make you feel? What kind of vision does it illicit in your imagination? Write down all thoughts and images stirred up in your mind and heart by the word)

Relevant Verses:

My Action Plan

What will I need to leave behind from the past or the past season?

What will help me gain momentum into next season?

What next steps will I have to implement to move forward effectively this next season?

Who has The Lord placed in my life for accountability? Who will I invite to hold me accountable to this action plan?

_____

_____

By _____ 20____, I will_____

_____

_____

_____

_____

_____

_____

_____

_____

_____

_____

_____

_____

_____

_____

_____

_____

_____

_____

_____

_____

Coming into alignment with the Church

It's important to know what the Lord is saying about this season, about the church and where He is leading us together as His people. Write down what the prophets are saying about this upcoming season.

As a body, we need to move in the same direction to move forward. Reflect on what you've heard from the prophets. How is what God is doing in you and through you fit?

What adjustments in my life or lifestyle will I need to make in order to move in alignment with the Body of Christ?

Monthly Check-in: January

What is God doing in me?

What is God doing through me?

How am I doing with my priorities?

How am I doing with my boundaries?

Take a moment to reflect and pray about what you have noticed this last month. What are some of the victories you have experienced?

What adjustments need to be made?

Notes

Monthly Check-in: February

What is God doing in me?

What is God doing through me?

How am I doing with my priorities?

How am I doing with my boundaries?

Take a moment to reflect and pray about what you have noticed this last month. What are some of the victories you have experienced?

What adjustments need to be made?

Notes

Monthly Check-in: March

What is God doing in me?

What is God doing through me?

How am I doing with my priorities?

How am I doing with my boundaries?

Take a moment to reflect and pray about what you have noticed this last month. What are some of the victories you have experienced?

What adjustments need to be made?

Notes

Monthly Check-in: April

What is God doing in me?

What is God doing through me?

How am I doing with my priorities?

How am I doing with my boundaries?

Take a moment to reflect and pray about what you have noticed this last month. What are some of the victories you have experienced?

_____

_____

_____

_____

_____

_____

_____

_____

_____

_____

_____

_____

_____

_____

_____

_____

_____

_____

_____

_____

_____

_____

_____

_____

_____

What adjustments need to be made?

Notes

Monthly Check-in: May

What is God doing in me?

What is God doing through me?

How am I doing with my priorities?

How am I doing with my boundaries?

Take a moment to reflect and pray about what you have noticed this last month. What are some of the victories you have experienced?

What adjustments need to be made?

Notes

Monthly Check-in: June

What is God doing in me?

What is God doing through me?

How am I doing with my priorities?

How am I doing with my boundaries?

Take a moment to reflect and pray about what you have noticed this last month. What are some of the victories you have experienced?

_____

_____

_____

_____

_____

_____

_____

_____

_____

_____

_____

_____

_____

_____

_____

_____

_____

_____

_____

_____

_____

_____

_____

_____

_____

_____

What adjustments need to be made?

Notes

Monthly Check-in: July

What is God doing in me?

What is God doing through me?

How am I doing with my priorities?

How am I doing with my boundaries?

Take a moment to reflect and pray about what you have noticed this last month. What are some of the victories you have experienced?

What adjustments need to be made?

Notes

Monthly Check-in: August

What is God doing in me?

What is God doing through me?

How am I doing with my priorities?

How am I doing with my boundaries?

Take a moment to reflect and pray about what you have noticed this last month. What are some of the victories you have experienced?

What adjustments need to be made?

Notes

Monthly Check-in: September

What is God doing in me?

What is God doing through me?

How am I doing with my priorities?

How am I doing with my boundaries?

Take a moment to reflect and pray about what you have noticed this last month. What are some of the victories you have experienced?

What adjustments need to be made?

Notes

Monthly Check-in: October

What is God doing in me?

What is God doing through me?

How am I doing with my priorities?

How am I doing with my boundaries?

Take a moment to reflect and pray about what you have noticed this last month. What are some of the victories you have experienced?

What adjustments need to be made?

Notes

Monthly Check-in: November

What is God doing in me?

What is God doing through me?

How am I doing with my priorities?

How am I doing with my boundaries?

Take a moment to reflect and pray about what you have noticed this last month. What are some of the victories you have experienced?

_____

_____

_____

_____

_____

_____

_____

_____

_____

_____

_____

_____

_____

_____

_____

_____

_____

_____

_____

_____

_____

_____

_____

What adjustments need to be made?

Notes

Monthly Check-in: December

What is God doing in me?

What is God doing through me?

How am I doing with my priorities?

How am I doing with my boundaries?

Take a moment to reflect and pray about what you have noticed this last month. What are some of the victories you have experienced?

What adjustments need to be made?

Notes

Notes

Notes

Notes

Notes

Notes

Notes

Notes

Notes

Notes

FACING ZIKLAG:
TURNING CRISIS INTO CROWNS

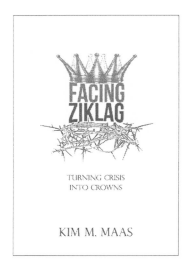

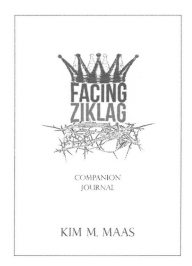

Crisis comes to everyone. It is a strategy devised by the enemy to keep you from your God-given destiny and often comes moments before the fulfilment of a prophetic promise. No one is immune. David was only twelve days from becoming king and receiving the crown prophesied to him by Samuel when he faced the events at Ziklag. The enemy hit him hard in a place and in a way he did not expect or anticipate, turning his world upside down. His decisions would be crucial to the outcome.

In this two-part booklet, you will discover how David's choices and response to God during the most pivotal moment in his life make all the difference in turning his crisis in to a crown. Gain the insight, keys, and strategy you need for facing, navigating, and overcoming your own Ziklag moments, with unwavering faith and courage.

The Facing Ziklag Companion Journal is a "must have" to help you work through your own Ziklag moment and move you forward to see your crisis turned into a crown.

PROPHETIC COMMUNITY
God's Call for All to Minister in His Gifts

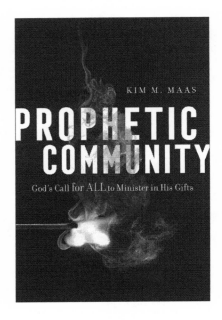

All God's people have been given the ability not only to hear his voice, but to speak his words. Yet some still believe that the gift of prophecy ceased with the death of the New Testament apostles. Others believe that gifts are reserved only for those specially anointed and appointed. Grounded in Scripture, international speaker and author Kim Maas will help you understand

· the history of the modern prophetic movement
· key misunderstandings and misconceptions about prophecy
· where prophetic community fits into God's kingdom plan

When the body of Christ recognizes that we are called to be a prophetic community, the voice of God will be released with fresh power in the church and the family, in the halls of justice and of education, in places of business and of leisure, and in the streets of every neighborhood, city, and nation. Lives will be changed. Communities will be transformed. Culture will be influenced. And history will be made.

ABOUT DR. KIM MAAS

Dr. Kim Maas is an international speaker and the Founder of Kim Maas Ministries, Inc. She has trained and equipped churches, ministries, and individuals to operate in the gift of prophecy in several nations and the United States. After a radical encounter with the Holy Spirit March 22, 1994, Kim left her twenty-two year nursing career to serve God full time. Her passion is to inspire, encourage and equip God's people to move forward toward fulfilling the call of God on their lives. This passion comes through in her preaching, leadership, writing, and everyday life. She is the president and C.E.O. of KIM MAAS MINISTRIES, Inc. and the founder and director of Women of Our Time (WOOT). In addition to speaking, preaching, and writing, she served as a pastor in the local church for over 12 years before becoming a full time itinerant minister. Kim earned a Doctorate in Ministry at United Theological Seminary and a Master of Divinity at King's University. Kim and her husband Mike live in Moorpark, CA. They have three grown children and five grandchildren.

For more information about Dr. Kim Maas or to invite her to speak at your next event visit: kimmaas.com

To follow her on twitter: @pkmaas
Or, write Kim at: hello@kimmaas.com

Dr. Kim Maas
P.O. Box 271
Moorpark, CA 93020

Made in the USA
Coppell, TX
15 July 2021